AWAY WITH THE FAIRIES

A guided meditation for children

Suitable for ages 2 and up

Dedicated to my love bugs Saoirse and Aisling,

my Hubbie, Mum, Dad, Sis

and to all my friends and family who supported me in making

this dream come true

Om Shanti Shanti Shanti

Once upon a time in a land far away,

Made of love, joy and light and games to play,

There were rainbows and sunshine and stars shining bright,

The fairies were dancing and singing of light.

You are there now with pure joy in your being,

Your heart plays the music of the beauty you're seeing,

Fairies surround you, stars shine on your powers,

And you dance and run freely through fields full of flowers.

You follow the rainbows and fly through the sky,

You feel all the colors, they make you so high,

Higher and higher and higher you go ,

The blue and the peace and the freedom and low

over meadows and castles and trees standing tall,

Over oceans and dolphins and mermaids that call.

Now you stop and you land in a magical ring,

Again Fairies surround you, they dance and they sing,

They sing for your soul and your spirit and light,

They dance for your joy, your heart flies like a kite.

Here you throw all your worries and troubles and woes,

Here you empty your sadness from your head to your toes,

Now the fairies they take all this sadness and strife,

And fill you with light and magic and life,

They sprinkle their dust and use all their powers,

You feel all the love growing in you like flowers.

You join your new friends and you dance and you play,

Till calm and content in the circle you lay,

You close both your eyes and peacefully sleep,

All the fairies and magic and memories you keep.

So you wake in this wonderful place called the present,

A gift you will treasure for you it is meant,

Your heart it still dances, your soul sings of love,

You thank all the stars as they shine from above.

You think of your loved ones and send them some light,

Your family, your friends, even those whom you fight,

You spread all these rainbows for world peace and health,

For you now know the meaning of love and true wealth.

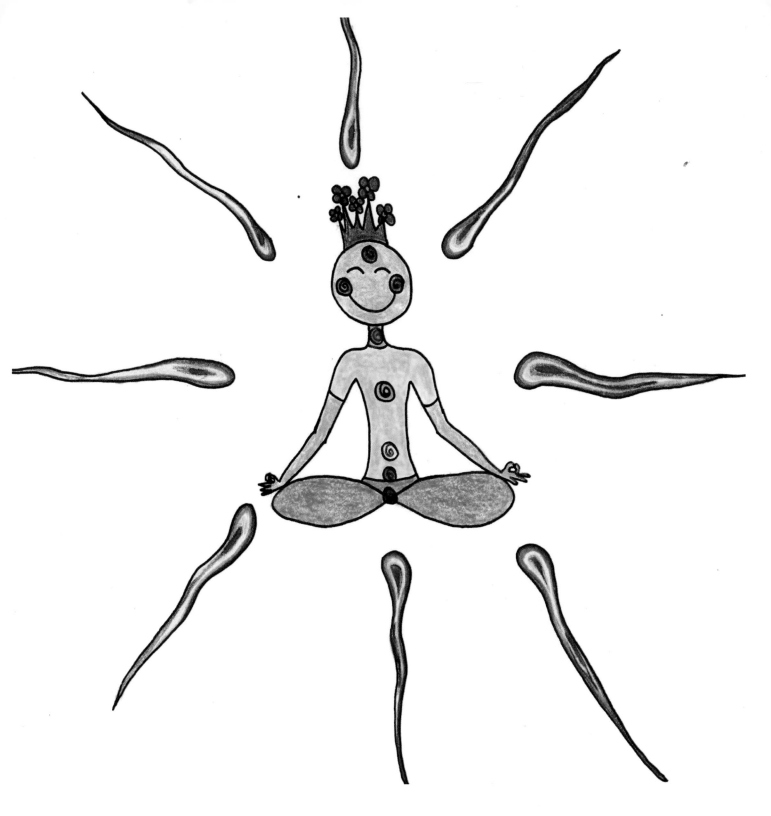

To the land of the Fairies you can return any day,

Till then, love and be happy and joyous and play!

First Edition

First Printing: 2016

ISBN-10:1523696524

+ISBN-13: 9781523696529

Visit our website www.lotuslearningpond.com

Aoife Kelly-Tate is from Cork, Ireland and now lives on a little ranch high in the Rocky Mountains of Crestone, Colorado. Aoife is a stay at home Mum of two young children and is also a highly qualified Yoga Teacher. She has years of experience teaching childrens' yoga classes and through her writing would like to continue to inspire children to meditate, visualize, relax and welcome more love, positivity and joy into their lives. She believes it is never too young to start meditation and Yoga and that introducing these practices in a fun way early in life provides a skill set and strong foundation that will be of huge benefit in the future.

Aoife is currently working on her next childrens' book which takes place in a magical enchanted forest. She looks forward to sharing it with you very soon!

To keep updated with Aoife's work please visit and "like" her facebook page – www.facebook.com/LotusLearningPond/

For a FREE AUDIO DOWNLOAD visit Aoife's website
www.lotuslearningpond.com

Dear 2018 Papi Mona and Sagey

thank you I love you so much
I loved the story with all the
colors and lovley amagintion that
was a good book it has a nice
story to it.

It had some rymes and lots of
interesting and lovley words like love
the saires are there to medetiut
us now that book it a good book
for bed times it will make you
have lovley dreams.

when I go to your house
I could read it to sagey
and I bet he will have nice

dreams.

I love you that lovley story has
Cleared all the bad stuff I have.

look at this chart
it as my sids I have
in my lovly brine

look this is
my brainy
thoughs

bad

	how that makes me ~~thoughts~~ feel
dreams	
harted house	sad
volcanos	
ship sinking	now its not ging to happen
some movies	very scard. I sometimes have night mars.
monsters	I feel tersied
wordrob	feel some thing is going to come out o f it.
slime	leans a monter clue
Books	some are pretty scary.
story's	from school
daddy	he goes to work
no~~XXX~~	more,
I	have
an~X	Ghost are in thes are

Good

	how it maks me seel
dreams	
goin to north pole	happy
sining santa	Amezing
My scarley	I love them
you	you make me shine
rain bows	so coterful
this book	refleces my mind.
other good books	Cool
my srinds	Cool verg
my teacher	she is kind
Jacob	cute to cute
mummy	she is my lovley srind
daddy	love him

that Just
me

Love from Suraya

is it croced or not. please mark it.

17 X 7 = 121

7 X
121 X

16300315R00016